LOOK CLOSER

DESERT LIFE

PHOTOGRAPHED BY
FRANK GREENAWAY

WRITTEN BY
BARBARA TAYLOR

DK

DORLING KINDERSLEY
LONDON . NEW YORK . STUTTGART

DK

A DORLING KINDERSLEY BOOK

Project editor Christiane Gunzi **Project art editor** Val Wright Heneghan

Editorial assistant Deborah Murrell **Designer** Julie Staniland
Design assistant Nicola Rawson

Production Louise Barratt
Illustrations Nick Hall, Nick Hewetson, Dan Wright
Additional editorial assistance Jill Somerscales

Managing editor Sophie Mitchell
Managing art editor Miranda Kennedy

Consultants
Barry Clarke, Andy Currant,
Theresa Greenaway, Paul Hillyard, Edward Wade

First published in Great Britain in 1992 by
Dorling Kindersley Limited
9 Henrietta Street
Covent Garden
London WC2E 8PS

A CIP catalogue for this book is available from the British Library.
ISBN 0 86318 772 2
Colour reproduction by Colourscan, Singapore
Printed and bound in Italy by New Interlitho, Milan

CONTENTS

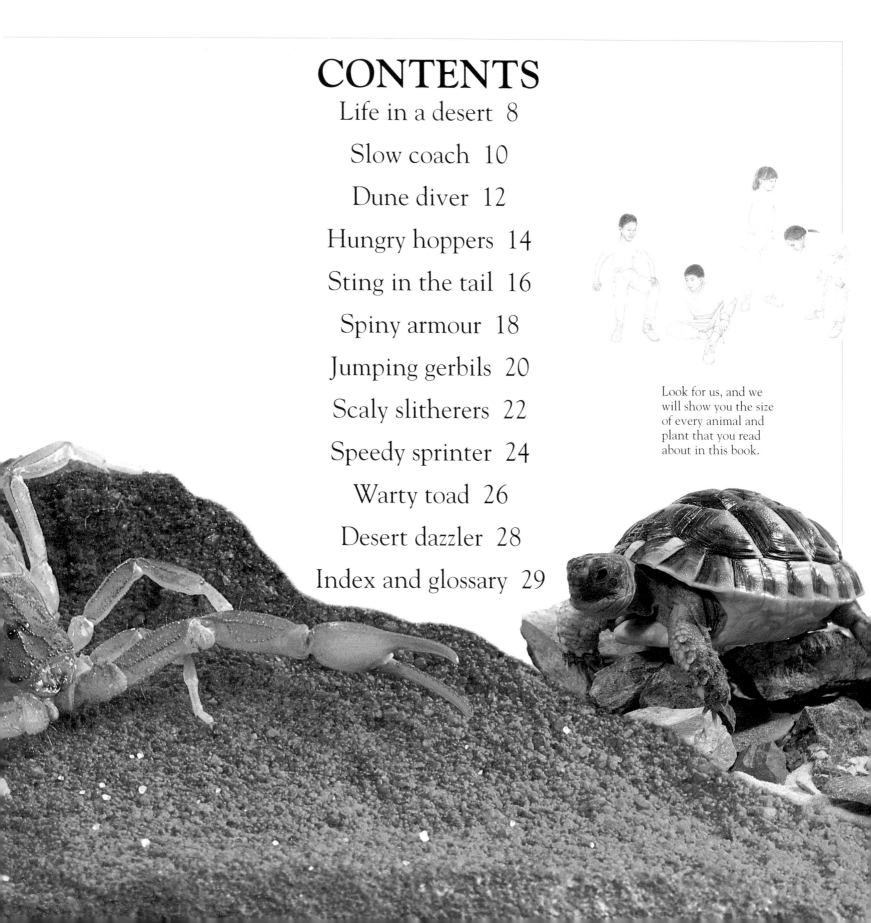

Look for us, and we will show you the size of every animal and plant that you read about in this book.

LIFE IN A DESERT

THE HOT DAYS AND COLD NIGHTS in the desert provide a harsh habitat for wildlife. Very little rain falls, and sometimes there is no rain at all for several years. The desert sands often seem lifeless. But look under a stone, or below the surface of the sand, and you will find all kinds of animals hiding from the heat of the sun. Insects, reptiles, birds, and mammals have all adapted to the desert conditions. Many plants and animals store water in their bodies to help them survive. Some plants flower and produce seeds only after rain has fallen. Snakes, scorpions, and other desert animals can survive without food and water for long periods. They often rest during the day to escape the heat, and some even sleep through the hottest months.

Grey banded king snake
Lampropeltis mexicana alterna
35 cm long

Diadem snake
Spalaerosophis diadema cliffordi
37 cm long

Green toad
Bufo viridis
8 cm long

Ground beetle
Thermophilum sexmaculatam
4 cm long

Locust nymph
Locustidae family
3 cm long

Cactus
*Mammillaria
magnimamma*
9 cm wide

Tortoise
Testudo graeca
shell 5 cm long

Cactus
Trichocereus
15 cm high

Cactus
*Mammillaria
hahniana*
9 cm high

Gerbil
*Meriones
unguiculatus*
body 8 cm long

Cactus
*Mammillaria
longiflora*
flowers 2.5 cm wide

Scorpion
*Androctonus
amoreuxi*
7 cm long

Sandfish
Scincus mitranus
14 cm long

Jewel wasp
*Ampulex
compressa*
2 cm long

SLOW COACH

TORTOISES USE UP VERY little energy in getting around, so they can survive long periods in the desert without food or drink. During the hottest months, they sometimes aestivate (sleep). Tortoises feed on dead animals, dung, and any plants which emerge after a fall of rain. They are reptiles, related to lizards, but unlike them they are too slow to catch prey or run away from enemies. In times of danger, the tortoise pulls its head back inside its shell for protection. Females lay eggs in a hole in the sand. The young tortoises break out of the shells using the horny tooth on their snouts. They have to fend for themselves as soon as they hatch, and many do not survive to become adults because they are attacked by birds of prey.

GUESS WHAT?
Many tortoises live for more than 100 years, and sometimes they live for up to 200 years.

ARMOUR-PLATING
The tortoise's shell is made up of about 60 bony plates which are joined together to form a protective shield for the body. On top of the bony plates are large, horny scales called scutes. These make the shell very strong. The top part of the shell, called the carapace, is connected to the backbone and ribs, as well as to the lower part of the shell, called the plastron.

Mottled colours on the outside of the shell help to disguise the tortoise.

SCALY SKIN

The tortoise's body is too large and clumsy to avoid rocks and thorny desert plants, so its skin is covered with leathery scales to protect it. This also helps to stop it from losing too much moisture. The scales on the legs are very large, and they have a bony centre.

TOOTHLESS JAWS

Tortoises have no teeth. Instead, their jaws have a hard, horny rim which is strong enough to bite off pieces of plants. The tortoise cannot chew its food as humans can, so it must bite off pieces which are small enough to swallow whole.

The high, domed shell makes it hard for an enemy to fit the tortoise inside its jaws and crush it.

Scientists can tell roughly how old a tortoise is by studying the growth rings on the scutes.

A long neck for stretching out from the shell to reach for plants

A ridge of small scales helps to protect the eyes.

There are two nostrils on the tip of the snout. A tortoise's sense of smell is excellent.

There are extra tough scales on the legs, to protect the tortoise against sharp rocks.

These very short toes have long claws for gripping surfaces and for pulling the tortoise along.

DUNE DIVER

LYING JUST BELOW the surface of the desert, the sandfish is well protected from the heat of the sun, and from enemies such as birds and snakes. This unusual creature belongs to a group of lizards called skinks. It hunts for beetles and other insects, and travels over the sand dunes by moving its body from side to side, rather like a fish swimming in water. The sandfish moves about mainly in the cool of the early morning and evening, and rests during the hottest hours. In the colder months, it hibernates (sleeps) under the sand. Sandfish lay two eggs which hatch after about two months. The young sandfish take nearly two years to grow into adults.

GUESS WHAT?
When it senses danger, the sandfish can dive into loose sand and disappear from sight. Fat stored in the tail helps the lizard to survive when food is hard to find.

The sandfish digs in the sand with its long snout.

The scales fit closely together and lie flat on the body so that they do not slow the lizard down.

NOSE DIGGER

The sandfish's nose is long and chisel-shaped. This helps it to push the sand aside as it moves beneath the dunes. The nose is also useful when the sandfish is searching below the surface for insects and other small prey.

These strong jaws are for crunching up tough food, such as beetles with hard wing cases.

Fringed toes stop the feet from sinking into the soft dunes.

The pointed tail is a good shape for sliding through the sand.

The body is long, smooth, and streamlined so that it can slip easily through the sand.

This red colour matches the sands of the Arabian desert where this sandfish lives, and helps to disguise it from enemies.

The ear openings are small and low down on the head. This helps to stop sand from getting in the sandfish's ears.

BURIED ALIVE
When a sandfish breathes under the sand, only the underside of its body moves in and out. If the sides of the body could move, the sandfish would be able to breathe out, but not in, because of the sand pressing against its body.

TRICKY TAIL
There are weak points in the sandfish's tail bones so that the tail can break off when it is grasped by an enemy. The lizard slowly grows a new tail, but it does not have weak points like the old one, and cannot break off as easily.

HUNGRY HOPPERS

DESERT LOCUSTS are grasshoppers with short antennae (feelers). They sometimes fly together in such huge swarms that they block out the sunlight. Young desert locusts are called nymphs, or hoppers. They cannot fly because their wings are not yet fully developed, so they use their long back legs to hop across the desert, sometimes forming large groups called bands. Hoppers hatch from eggs buried in the sand. Their skin is hard and does not stretch as they grow. Instead, the hoppers have to moult (shed their skin) from time to time. After several weeks, the hoppers develop into adult locusts with four wings, and they can take to the air.

The antennae are sensitive to touch and scent. They are jointed and can bend.

There are simple eyes at the base of the antennae for detecting changes in the brightness of sunlight.

Compound eyes made up of lots of lenses help the locust to see up to three metres away.

WAXED JACKET
A waterproof layer of wax covers the hopper's body and helps to stop it from losing water in the hot, dry desert. This waxed jacket is protected by an outer layer of hard varnish. Hoppers and adult locusts never need to drink because they get all the water they need from the plants that they eat.

A hard collar protects the wide part of the body called the thorax.

The hopper rubs its legs against these veins on the wings to make a chirping sound.

Hoppers gather together in bands, and hop about on the sand. The more hoppers there are, the faster they all hop.

The hard mandibles (jaws) cut and grind up food such as grass. They work like human teeth, although they are outside the body.

These front legs hold food close to the mouth during feeding.

CHAMPION LEAPER
Young hoppers have long back legs, like adult locusts. When hoppers become adults, their legs are so powerful that they can leap up to ten times their own length. These long leaps help locusts to escape from predators such as snakes.

COURTSHIP CALL
To attract a female for mating, a male locust makes chirping sounds. He rubs a ridge of pegs on the top part of his back leg against stiff veins on the front wing. Even hoppers have these special ridges on their legs.

GUESS WHAT?
A swarm of locusts can contain millions of individuals. Adult locusts often fly for thousands of miles, and they devastate huge areas of crops when they land to eat.

ON THE MARCH
Large bands of hoppers sometimes cover the desert sands for several square kilometres. They rest during the heat of the day, and usually feed in the cool of the morning and evening. A band of hoppers may move as much as a kilometre and a half in one day.

Each time the hopper moults, its wings grow bigger.

Long back legs with strong muscles for leaping

A special ridge of pegs on each leg for making the chirping sounds

Sharp spines on each leg deter snakes from attacking. They also help the hopper to grip on to plant stems.

The abdomen has many segments so it can bend.

When this female hopper becomes an adult, she will use the end of her abdomen to dig a hole in the sand for her eggs.

Tough, hard feet with hooks for holding on to rocks and plants

STING IN THE TAIL

THE SCORPION IS ONE of the most dangerous creatures in the desert. This desert scorpion can kill a human with its poisonous sting, although it usually only stings to protect itself and to kill its prey. Scorpions are well suited to life in the dry desert because they can go without water for several months. They can also survive for more than a year without eating any food. Scorpions are active mainly at night. During the day, they hide away in burrows or under stones, where it is cool and damp. The female gives birth to several young, which look like tiny versions of their parents. When the young have moulted once, they leave their mother and go off to fend for themselves. Young scorpions take about a year to develop into adults.

The tail is made up of a narrow section of the abdomen.

Poison comes from two glands inside the swollen part of the sting.

The scorpion arches its tail over its head and injects poison through the sharp tip of the sting. The poison paralyzes the victim so it cannot move.

The sting tip is long and sharp for piercing the victim's skin.

Joints between the segments of the tail allow it to bend easily.

The sandy colouring is a good disguise when the scorpion has to move about during the day.

Hairs on the legs detect the movements of other creatures.

HAIRY LEGS
Stiff hairs on the scorpion's legs detect tiny vibrations (movements) in the air. The time it takes for the vibrations to travel from the front legs to the back legs helps the scorpion to work out the position of its food, a mate, or an enemy.

GUESS WHAT?
Sometimes the female scorpion kills and eats the male scorpion after they have mated.

JOINTED JAWS

Scorpions feed on insects, centipedes, spiders, and lizards. Strong, jointed jaws outside the mouth pull food to pieces and crush it to a soft pulp. Special fluids from the stomach help to digest the food. The scorpion then sucks up the juices from its victim's body into its small mouth.

DEADLY INJECTION

Most scorpions are harmless to people and their stings are no more dangerous than a wasp sting. But the poison from the sting of this scorpion destroys the nerves in the victim's body and can kill a human in a few hours.

Scorpions have four pairs of eyes, but they cannot see well. Their eyes are small and simple, so they find their food mainly by touch and smell instead.

These jointed jaws tear the scorpion's food into small pieces.

CLAWED HANDS

The scorpion has two special leg-like pedipalps, with strong pincers on the ends which grab and hold food. Male and female scorpions also hold each other by their pincers during their courtship dance.

Strong pincers for catching food

SPINY ARMOUR

A CACTUS CAN SURVIVE with very little water, and some kinds can live for years without any water at all. Cactus roots spread out near the surface so that they can soak up moisture from dew or brief rainstorms. Most plants lose water through tiny breathing holes in their leaves and stems. But cacti have developed spines rather than leaves, and they have fewer holes in their stems, so less water can escape. Inside the stem, there are cells which store water like a sponge. New cacti grow from branches, called offsets, which sprout near the base of the parent cacti. They also grow from seeds which develop if one cactus flower receives pollen from another of the same kind.

GUESS WHAT?
These small, round cacti only grow to a few centimetres high. But the tall one can grow up to a metre high if the conditions are right.

PRICKLY SPINES
The tough, sharp spines protect the cactus in many ways. They help to shade the stem, and collect dew in the early morning. The dew runs down to the soil, where the roots absorb it. The spines also trap a layer of air around the plant so less moisture is blown away by the wind. Animals that try to eat the cactus are soon put off by the prickly spines.

Fine hairs shield the stem against strong sunlight.

RARE BLOOMS
These brightly coloured cactus flowers attract insects such as bees and beetles. The insects feed on the nectar made by the flowers and carry pollen from one flower to another. When a cactus flower opens, lots of precious water escapes from the petals. So cacti usually flower for only a few days each year.

There are bags of yellow pollen called anthers in the centre of the flower.

The hooks on the spines of these cacti give them the popular name of fishhook cactus.

White spines reflect sunlight away from the cactus.

These ribs can expand to store water.

CONCERTINA STEM

The stems of cacti like this one are folded into pleats which expand and contract like a concertina. This helps the cactus to store as much water as possible when it rains. The stems contain up to 90 per cent water. Without its pleats, the cactus would split open.

The green colour in the stem is due to chlorophyll, which the plant uses to trap energy from sunlight to make its own food.

The stem has a thick, waxy surface to stop water from escaping.

SPIKY SPOKES

Cacti have very short side branches called areoles. The spines grow out of the areoles in clusters like the spokes of a wheel, so that they cast as much shade as possible. There are extra spines on the top of the cactus to protect the delicate growing tip.

Extra spines on the top of the plant

Spines grow out of small side branches called areoles.

JUMPING GERBILS

THESE AGILE MONGOLIAN GERBILS jump and
scurry about in the desert in the cool of the night.
During the day, they usually hide away from the
dry heat in burrows underground. Gerbils
never drink. They get all the water they need
from their food. At night, when gerbils
come out for food, the seeds they find are
dampened by the dew. Gerbils take their
food back to their burrow to eat. These
seeds take in more moisture from the damp
air in the burrow. The female Mongolian
gerbil visits another burrow to mate with a
male, but returns to the safety of her own burrow
to give birth to her young. The young are born with
fur, and their eyes are closed. Like other mammals,
they feed on their mother's milk for the first few weeks.
The adult males in the burrow help to look after the
young until they are old enough to fend for themselves.

The large eyes can see in the dark and they spot danger in time for the gerbil to leap quickly away.

Gerbils hold food in their front paws while they eat it.

This pale-coloured fur disguises the gerbil against the desert sand.

FOOD STORES
Mongolian gerbils eat the seeds of
desert plants. These plants flower and
produce seeds only after brief
rainstorms. When there is plenty of
food available, gerbils store seeds
in their burrows. Special pouches
in their cheeks help them to
carry many seeds at once.
They can eat these later when
food is hard to find.

The special pouches in the cheeks stretch so that the gerbil can carry lots of food in its mouth.

Large back feet help the gerbil to stand upright so that it can search for enemies.

TRICKY TAIL

This gerbil's beige-coloured coat matches the colour of the sand where it lives. If it comes out during the day, predators such as birds and foxes cannot spot it easily. A tuft of darker fur on the end of the tail acts as a decoy, so that if an enemy sees the gerbil at all, it will attack its tail. The tail can break off completely if this happens, but it cannot grow again.

GUESS WHAT?
Gerbils are great hoarders of food. One Mongolian gerbil was found with 20 kg of seeds stored in its burrow.

There is a dark tuft on the end of the tail to attract enemies away from the animal's head.

KANGAROO HOP

Gerbils have fur on the undersides of their feet to protect them from the hot desert sand. They can also make huge leaps on their long back legs so their feet do not have to touch the sand very often. The gerbil uses its long tail for balance and to change direction as it bounds along like a tiny kangaroo.

Powerful back legs to push the gerbil upwards and forwards through the air

Large ears allow the gerbil to hear enemies, such as foxes and snakes.

The white fur on the belly reflects heat, and this helps the gerbil to keep cool.

Sturdy front legs to take the weight of the body on landing

These long, sensitive whiskers help the gerbil to feel its way in the dark and underground.

SCALY SLITHERERS

WITH THEIR WATERTIGHT SKIN to keep in moisture, snakes survive well in the desert. Like other reptiles, they need the heat of the sun to warm their bodies and give them the energy to move. Snakes can survive for a long time without eating. This is useful in the desert where their food of birds, small mammals, and reptiles is often hard to find. Female snakes lay soft-shelled eggs under stones or below the surface of the sand, where it is warm and damp, and then leave them. As soon as the eggs have hatched, the young snakes can fend for themselves and find prey, such as small lizards.

BUILT FOR SPEED

Snakes are streamlined for speed, so they can move quickly and quietly to escape from enemies and catch their prey. A snake wriggles along in a series of S-shaped curves. The scales on the underside grip the sand so that the snake does not slip.

STRETCHY SKIN

The king snake's skin expands when the snake swallows a meal larger than itself. Like other snakes, it moults as it grows. About a week before it moults, the snake goes blind and the eyes look blue and cloudy. They clear again about two days before the snake moults.

The skin is made up of thickened, horny scales, which overlap each other. The skin stretches easily between the scales.

This king snake has a similar colour and pattern to the poisonous coral snake. Enemies may think that this king snake is poisonous too.

FORKED TONGUE

A snake's forked tongue picks up scent particles from the air and carries them to a special part of the mouth called the Jacobson's organ. The snake builds up a picture of its surroundings based on different scents. This helps it to track down food and avoid enemies. This special sense helps to make up for the snake's weak hearing and eyesight.

GUESS WHAT?
Snakes do not have external (outside) ears, so they do not hear sounds which travel through the air, as humans do. Instead, snakes can pick up vibrations through the ground.

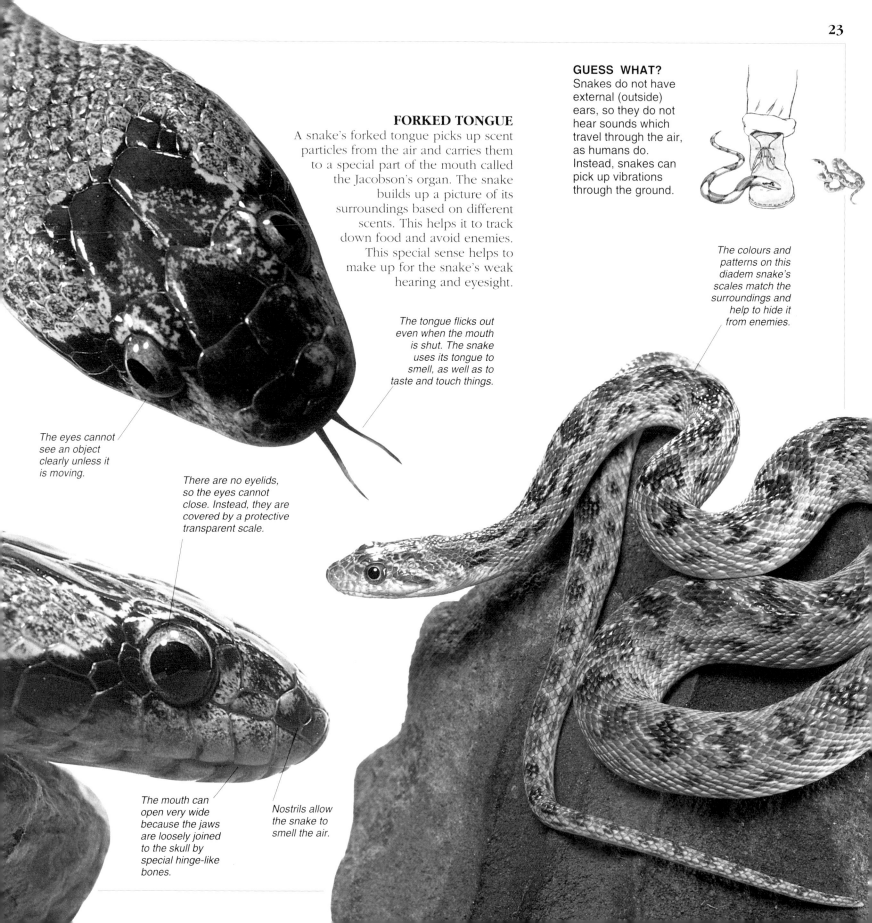

The colours and patterns on this diadem snake's scales match the surroundings and help to hide it from enemies.

The tongue flicks out even when the mouth is shut. The snake uses its tongue to smell, as well as to taste and touch things.

The eyes cannot see an object clearly unless it is moving.

There are no eyelids, so the eyes cannot close. Instead, they are covered by a protective transparent scale.

The mouth can open very wide because the jaws are loosely joined to the skull by special hinge-like bones.

Nostrils allow the snake to smell the air.

SPEEDY SPRINTER

THIS GROUND BEETLE is as fierce a hunter as it looks, chasing after other insects and spiders on its long legs. It cannot fly because its wings are stuck together, but it can run very fast and has good eyesight for spotting prey. Food is often scarce in the desert, but ground beetles can survive for months without eating. There are four stages in a beetle's life. First, the female lays eggs, which hatch into larvae (grubs). Each larva moults three times as it grows. Eventually the larva becomes a pupa, and its whole body changes shape until it finally turns into an adult beetle. This kind of ground beetle is sometimes called a domino beetle because of the white spots on its black body. The bold pattern warns enemies not to attack. If they do, the beetle may spray them with a special chemical that burns.

BODY ON STILTS
The ground beetle has three pairs of long, slender legs, all about the same size. They help the beetle to run fast when chasing prey or escaping from enemies. They also hold the beetle's body high above the hot desert sand.

The large head allows space for the oversized jaw muscles.

The large compound eyes have many separate lenses. These give the beetle the keen eyesight it needs for hunting.

The long antennae (feelers) are joined to the side of the head. They pick up vibrations and scents from the air.

The large, strong mandibles are perfect for chopping up food, such as other insects and their larvae.

JAGGED JAWS
The ground beetle grabs its prey with its pointed, toothed mandibles (jaws). Then it uses its other mouthparts to tear the food into pieces. Once an animal is caught, it has little chance of escape.

Hooks on the legs and feet help the beetle to grip on to sand and rocks without slipping.

HAIRY LEGS
Tiny hairs on the legs and body are sensitive to vibrations (movements) in the air. This helps the beetle to detect enemies and search for food or a mate.

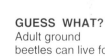

GUESS WHAT?
Adult ground beetles can live for several years. This one is at least six years old.

OUTSIDE SKELETON
Like all insects, the ground beetle has an outer skeleton called an exoskeleton. It is made of a hard substance called chitin. This adult beetle has now reached its full size and will not moult again.

Rows of dots along the wing cases help scientists to tell this beetle apart from other kinds.

The wing cases are stuck together.

A hard exoskeleton protects the beetle's fragile body.

This ground beetle can squirt a jet of nasty burning chemicals from the rear end of its body to deter enemies.

The body is flexible between each segment and it can bend easily.

Hairs on the body and legs

WARTY TOAD

DURING THE DAY, the green toad hides from the heat of the sun under a rock or in the sand, where it is cool. The toad comes out to feed at night, using its long, sticky tongue to catch ants and other small insects. Toads survive well in hot, dry areas because they never need to drink. Instead, they absorb moisture from food and through their skin. Green toads have small bumps on their skin which produce a special slime called mucus to keep them moist. There are also larger warts all over the body containing poison. This poison protects the toad from predators. Green toads that live in hot, dry, desert areas only breed after a rainstorm because, like other amphibians, they need to lay their eggs in pools of water. The eggs develop into tadpoles, and after about a year they become fully-grown toads.

TOAD TALK
Toads hear well and have a flat, round eardrum on each side of the head, just below the poison gland. Toads make many different kinds of sounds for scaring off enemies and for communicating with each other when they are looking for a mate.

Green toads have a third eyelid which slides across the eye for protection when they are under the soil or sand.

The pupil in the middle of each eyeball can close to a slit in really bright sunlight.

TOOTHLESS WONDER
The toad has no teeth and swallows its food whole. Each time it swallows, its eyeballs sink down into the mouth to help force food down the throat.

MOUTH BREATHER
To pump air in and out of its lungs, the toad pushes the lower part of its mouth up and down and moves its throat muscles in and out. The toad can also breathe through its moist skin.

Green toads can breathe through their skin.

GUESS WHAT?
An adult female green toad often lays more than 10,000 eggs at one time.

Each foot has fingers which the toad uses to wipe dirt off its food before eating it.

There is a round, flat eardrum on each side of the head called a tympanum. These eardrums pick up vibrations in the air.

The large lump behind the eye is a large poison gland called the paratoid gland.

These large, knobbly warts produce poison.

POISONOUS WARTS
The brightly coloured patterns on the toad's skin act as a disguise and also warn enemies that it is poisonous. Predators soon learn to leave the toad alone. The poisons are produced in a special gland behind the eye and also in the large warts all over the skin.

Bright colours and patterns to deter enemies

DESERT DAZZLER

LIKE SEVERAL OTHER WASPS, the dazzling jewel wasp is a solitary creature. It does not form large colonies like the familiar black and yellow striped wasps which buzz around us in the summer. Adult jewel wasps feed on the sweet nectar in flowers, but their larvae (grubs) are parasites (animals which live off another living creature). The female wasp stings a cockroach to paralyze it so that it cannot escape, then drags it into a hole in the sand, and lays a single egg on it. The cockroach dies, but its flesh stays fresh for weeks because the poison in the sting contains an antiseptic to stop the flesh rotting. The larva hatches from the egg about three days later. It has no legs because its meals are provided and it does not need to move to find food. When it has eaten enough food it turns into a pupa, and about three weeks later emerges as an adult wasp.

BUG EYES

Huge compound eyes, made up of many separate lenses, provide the jewel wasp with excellent eyesight. The eyes are set on each side of the head, which can turn freely. This means that the wasp can look all around itself for enemies such as lizards, or cockroaches for its young to feed on.

The two pairs of wings hook together during flight, and fold back across the body when not in use.

Close-up, you can see tiny hairs on the insect's body. These help to absorb heat, which the wasp needs in order to stay active.

These orange-coloured legs warn enemies that the wasp is poisonous.

Hooks on each leg grip on to the cockroach.

The antennae pick up scents in the air and help the wasp to find its prey.

GUESS WHAT?
The jewel wasp's sting developed over thousands of years from the egg-laying tube, so only females are capable of stinging.

STRONG GRIP
The female jewel wasp digs a hole for her egg by moving grains of sand with her strong jaws and kicking away loose sand with her legs. She also grips her cockroach victim firmly in her jaws while injecting venom into its body from the sting on the tip of her abdomen. Adult jewel wasps feed on nectar, so they use their jaws mainly when preparing a home for their young.

A small cockroach like this one is easy prey. Sometimes a wasp will choose a cockroach almost twice its own size.

INDEX

GLOSSARY

Abdomen *the rear part of the body*
Aestivate *to rest or sleep during the hot months of the year*
Amphibians *animals such as frogs, which live both on land and in water*
Antennae *a pair of feelers*
Camouflage *the colours or patterns of an animal which match its background*
Exoskeleton *an outer covering on the body, made of a substance called chitin*
Larvae *grubs, which eventually develop into adult insects*
Mandibles *jaws*

Mammal *a warm-blooded animal such as a mouse or a rabbit*
Moult *to shed the skin or exoskeleton*
Mucus *a slimy, often poisonous substance which certain animals produce*
Pupa *the resting stage between a larva and an adult insect*
Reptile *a cold-blooded animal such as a turtle or a snake*
Thorax *the front part of the body, containing the heart and lungs*
Vibrations *tiny movements in air, in water, or underground*